UNDER THE GUN:
THE MANUAL

UNDER THE GUN:
THE MANUAL

Fundamentals of Handgun Disarming

James Miller

Paladin Press
Boulder, Colorado

Also by James Miller:
Under the Gun: Fundamentals of Handgun Disarming (video)

Under the Gun: The Manual
Fundamentals of Handgun Disarming
by James Miller

Copyright © 2006 by James Miller

ISBN 13: 978-1-58160-549-5
Printed in the United States of America

Published by Paladin Press, a division of
Paladin Enterprises, Inc.
Gunbarrel Tech Center
7077 Winchester Circle
Boulder, Colorado 80301 USA
+1.303.443.7250

Direct inquiries and/or orders to the above address.

PALADIN, PALADIN PRESS, and the "horse head" design are trademarks belonging to Paladin Enterprises and registered in United States Patent and Trademark Office.

All rights reserved. Except for use in a review, no portion of this book may be reproduced in any form without the express written permission of the publisher.

Neither the author nor the publisher assumes any responsibility for the use or misuse of information contained in this book.

Visit our Web site at www.paladin-press.com

Contents

Chapter 1
Prior to Training 3

Chapter 2
Principles and Concepts 7

Chapter 3
Training Evolutions 23

Chapter 4
Empty-Hand Responses: Frontal Attacks 33

Chapter 5
Empty-Hand Responses: Rear Attacks 47

Chapter 6
Armed Responses 63

Dedication

This book is dedicated to the memory of the men and women of law enforcement who make the ultimate sacrifice every year.

No greater love has a man than this, that he lay down his life for his friends.

—John 15:13

Acknowledgments

I would like to thank several people who both encouraged and supported this project. First, my wife, Jane, who helped with everything; Jeff West for acting as a bad guy and taking the lumps; Sheila Hullihen for her photographic expertise; my father for his much needed help with all things computer; John Kelley for all the bruises through the years; Frank Wagoner for his assistance in the initial phases of this project; some old teammates (who wish to remain anonymous) for their logistical support; Mike Janich for his encouragement; and last, but certainly not least, James Keating for his encouragement and support of this and other projects. I am grateful to you all!

Warning

The handgun disarming techniques depicted in this book can be extremely dangerous. It is not the intent of the author or publisher to encourage readers to attempt any of them without proper professional supervision and training.

The author, publisher, and distributors of this book disclaim any liability from any damage or injuries of any type that a reader or user of information contained within this book may incur from the use of said information. This book is *for academic study only.*

Introduction

Disarming an assailant who is armed with a handgun is not an act to be taken lightly. You will have only one chance and the margin for error is hair-thin. A disarm should be attempted when the only other options are to be shot or to watch another innocent party be shot. The training that makes it possible to perform a disarm is as serious as the situation for which you are preparing.

Over the years, even the good disarms I've seen taught have rarely been taken past the introductory phase. This book is not meant to be the last word on disarming techniques. Instead, the training methods shown here can be used as a test and evaluation method for techniques that are already known as well. They can also be used as methods for real events.

Remember that when training to real-world capability, there are risks of injury that you must assume. These can be diminished through the use of personal protective equipment, safety protocols, and the right mindset. The risks, however, can never be completely eliminated.

chapter 1

Prior to Training

Prior to beginning any weapon disarming training, several safety considerations must be taken into account. The first is that no loaded firearms, live ammunition, or live blades of any kind are allowed in the training area. A recommended procedure is to have a preparation room outside the training area. Trainees can unload or secure their firearms along with any spare ammunition, loaded magazines, speedloaders, and live blades. Anyone found with any of these items on their person in the training area should be removed immediately.

The second consideration is the use of personal protective equipment.

Initially, you will need nothing beyond a dummy gun and possibly a pair of gloves for each trainee. As your training evolutions progress, you will need to add safety glasses, chest protection, full face shields, throat wraps, a cup and supporter, and training knives.

Equipment for all training evolutions.

The safety equipment required depends on where you are in your training cycle as well as what type of equipment you are using during the stress inoculation portion of the training (more on that later). For safety reasons, is *not* recommended that real firearms be used during training. There may be rare situations in which this becomes necessary. If you must use real firearms in training, the following procedure is recommended:

1. Unload all firearms in the preparation area.

2. Prior to practicing any techniques, one partner will lock the slide of the pistol to the rear or open the action on the revolver and visually and physically inspect the chamber and magazine well or cylinder for ammunition. When doing this, you should look for ammunition, not an empty space indicating the absence of ammunition. This is because the eye tends to see what it wants to see.

Prior to Training

If you are forced to use a real firearm in training, you must ensure that it is unloaded.

First, point it in a safe direction.

Second, remove the magazine.

Third, lock the slide to the rear.

Fourth, physically and visually inspect the magazine well and chamber.

3. The trainee then hands the firearm to his partner, who repeats the process.

4. The firearm is then handed back to the first trainee, who again checks the firearm for live ammunition. Prior to closing the action, he will insert a chamber block if one is available.

5. Any time the weapon leaves the *immediate control* of the training partners, this procedure is repeated.

This procedure may seem tedious, but law enforcement officers are killed or injured every year in legitimate training exercises while using firearms they *thought* were unloaded. We do not need to add to their numbers.

Everyone involved in training is a safety officer. Anyone who sees something that could result in an injury needs to know that they can and should stop the exercise and correct the situation.

Live environment training, as a rule, is essential to build real-world skills and capabilities. There is an exception to that rule, however: Don't train in a location where you can be seen or heard by the public. If you ignore this advice and decide to have a training session at the local park, back alley, or the beach, expect a visit from local law enforcement and expect to have live weapons pointed at you.

chapter 2

Principles and Concepts

RANGE

Range is crucial in successful handgun disarming. We are concerned with the distance between ourselves and the opponent's weapon, not the distance between us and the opponent himself. Our primary goal is to attack the *weapon*. The weapon is what makes our opponent's assault lethal and it must be our main priority. A secondary goal is to attack our opponent's ability to *use* the weapon. Even if you can hit like a heavyweight champ or an angry kung fu master, your assailant is likely to survive long enough to shoot you, either intentionally or reflexively if you forget this: We need a clear path to the weapon.

There are three ranges with which we are concerned. They are:

- *From body contact out to arm's reach.* If the weapon is within this range and you have a clear path to it, disarming is possible.

- *Just beyond arm's reach to about five steps.* If the gun is beyond your reach by as little as one step, you will likely be shot for your trouble if you attempt to disarm your attacker. From one step out to about five, most people can hit a man-sized target with point shooting alone.
- *Beyond five steps.* In this range our ability to evade and escape, or to evade and bring our own firearm into play as we move to cover, increases.

REACTION TIME

Reaction time is the next thing we need to consider—both our attacker's and our own. If your attacker presents his weapon and immediately fires, before you can react, then you can dispense with anything further because you have been shot. However, if we train to move off the line of force the moment we see a weapon presented to us, we may still prevail. If we are taken by surprise and not shot immediately, then our assailant wants something. We can now be proactive.

Many will state that the fastest human reaction time is .25 second. What often isn't said is that this is an average time to respond to an unknown stimulus with an unplanned response. If your assailant has already decided to shoot if you resist or fail to comply, this reaction time drops dramatically. In some informal testing, I have seen times as low as .11 second, with .15 to .18 second being common.

The OODA Loop

The best way to explain the difference is the OODA Loop, first described by the great fighter pilot John Boyd. The loop describes the decision-making process all humans make daily whenever confronted with a choice. The loop consists of four elements: Observe, Orient, Decide, and Act. We must observe or be aware of something to react to it. We must then orient

Principles and Concepts

ourselves properly toward the stimulus. Once oriented, we must decide what actions we are going to take. Finally, we must act. Once we have acted, the cycle begins anew as we observe the result of our actions, orient ourselves anew to the results, decide if we need to act further, and finally act on the new situation. As you can see, if your assailant is already observing you, is oriented toward you, and has decided what he will do if you do not comply, all he needs to do is act. Three-fourths of the OODA Loop have been completed.

There are several lessons in this. First, there are no feints, no moves to draw a reaction. When you act, you must act decisively and aggressively to end the threat.

Second, you must train yourself to get inside your opponent's OODA Loop. Once you have a solid grasp of the techniques you must begin training yourself to distract your opponent. We do this by giving him something else to think about. Pain distractions need to be done *after* the muzzle is deflected away from us and is at least partially under our control. Mental distractions can be done prior to this.

For example, if you are the target of a robbery attempt, asking your assailant if he would like your car keys as well as your wallet—as you're ready to disarm him—may buy you precious time as he thinks of a response. You must, however, train yourself *now* to say these things; under stress, you may very well not be able to think of it. Program the dialogue into your mind now through hard training and it will be there for you when you need it.

When preparing to disarm an assailant, understand that the firearm will likely discharge during the action. Statistics show that this occurs in about 90 percent of disarming attempts.[1] Expect this to occur so you won't be startled when it does. You also need to understand that more than just the bullet comes out of the muzzle as a weapon discharges. Hot gases, ash, and unburned powder follow the round in the form of muzzle flash. If you are struck in the eyes by this discharge, you have to be mentally prepared to fight through the pain and vision impairment.

You must also consider that in about 30 percent of all disarming attempts, the defender (that's you) is shot.[2] That's the bad news; the good news is that the fatality rate for *all* shootings is around 3 percent. Of that 3 percent, 75 percent of those shootings are self-inflicted accidents and 23 percent are suicides. This leaves us with 2 percent of the original 3 that are intentional shootings.[3] The lesson here is that, even if you are shot, if you are still conscious and can move, *fight!* Your odds of survival are excellent. *Do not quit!*

TWO DIRECTIONS AT ONCE

The concept of two directions at once is this: human beings can only resist effectively in one direction at a time. Knowing this, if you move an individual or part of an individual in two directions at once, you dramatically increase your odds of success. Let's look at a common wristlock to illustrate this. It goes by several names—*kote gaeshi*, the reverse wristlock, the bent wrist press, or the wrist out turn.

Normally, when this lock is taught, the student is told to grab his opponent's hand by the thumb side, turn the palm up to the sky, bend the hand toward the inner forearm, and then turn the hand outward away from the centerline of the body.

There are several variations on how this is done, along with the footwork required to take your adversary to the ground and control him or to break his wrist where he stands. The important thing to look at for our immediate purpose is that if you perform the lock in the steps as described, your partner or opponent can stop you merely by locking his wrist with muscular tension. It then becomes a matter of who is stronger as to whether you will succeed in making the lock work, as long as he doesn't decide to hit you in the interim.

Grasp your partner's hand by the thumb side.

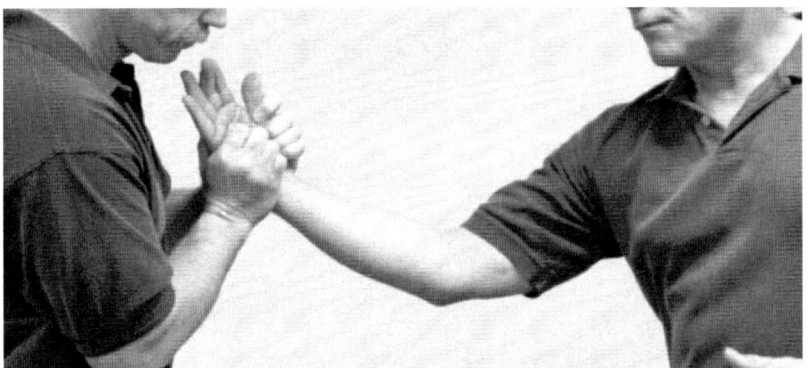

Turn his palm up and grasp the little finger side of his hand with your other hand

Turn the hand out.

Now, try the same lock again, but this time, bend the hand in toward the forearm and simultaneously twist the wrist out. You will notice that your training partner will have a much more difficult time resisting your actions.

SPIRALING LIMBS

Spiraling limbs describes the principle that humans do not track well on circles. Have your training partner hold his arm straight out from the shoulder and make a fist. Now push his arm in a straight line in any direction as he resists. You will find it difficult to move his arm. Now, have him do the same thing with his other arm. This time, grasp his fist with your fingertips and move his fist in circles randomly. You should find that he is easy to move in any direction you choose. This is useful in applying techniques such as a straight-arm bar. If you try to push your partner to the ground, he may be able to resist you. If you try again and this time make circles with the arm you have locked, you will find it easier to take your partner to the ground.

Finally, before we get into the specifics of the disarms, I advise you to learn to use a handgun combatively. Even if you never carry one for defense, learn to use one. If attacked by more than one assailant, you may be able to turn an opponent's weapon back on your adversaries. Another reason is that once you are familiar with weapons, the fear of them leaves. You must always respect the weapon, but *fear* of the weapon will clog your mind. Lastly, if you do disarm an opponent and you know how to handle firearms, you are less likely to shoot yourself in the aftermath.

THE DISARMING FORMULA

The final thing you must understand before we begin the techniques is the disarming formula. There are four steps to any successful disarm. They are:

Principles and Concepts

- Clear
- Control
- Disarm
- Disable

Regardless of the techniques you use, if these four elements are present in this order, the disarm has an excellent chance of success. If the disarm does not contain these elements, or if they are employed out of order, your chances of success become a roll of the dice.

Clearing involves getting yourself off the line of fire. You must clear the weapon's muzzle from your body. There are three ways you can achieve this. You can simply shift your body, you can push the gun away from you, or you can do a combination of the two.

It is recommended that you shift your body off line as you push the muzzle away from you. The first method, shifting your body, is very fast. However, you will have very little room between you and the muzzle if and when the gun discharges. The second method, pushing the gun aside, puts more distance between you and the muzzle, but it is slower and forces you to push the muzzle across perhaps half your body. By shifting and pushing simultaneously, you can quickly clear yourself and create a large gap between the muzzle (and what comes out of it) and your tender flesh.

There is some disagreement concerning to which direction you should clear. In other words, do you push the muzzle to the inside line or to the outside line? Some advocate clearing to the inside only. Those who advise this believe that clearing to the outside pushes the gun to the opponent's opposite hand and allows him to pass the gun and fire using that hand. They also will tell you that clearing to the inside causes the opponent's hand to open slightly, creating a small advantage for you.

The assailant presents a handgun to the defender's torso.

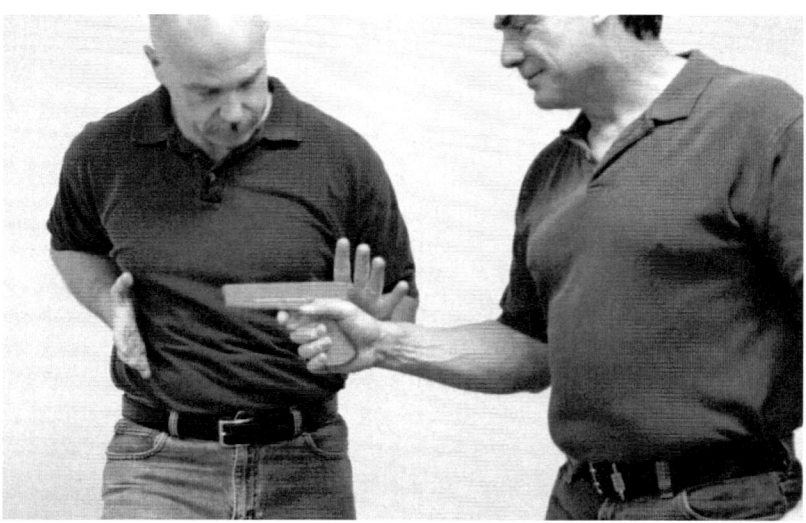

The defender clears by snapping his body sideways only.

Principles and Concepts

The assailant presents a handgun to the defender's torso.

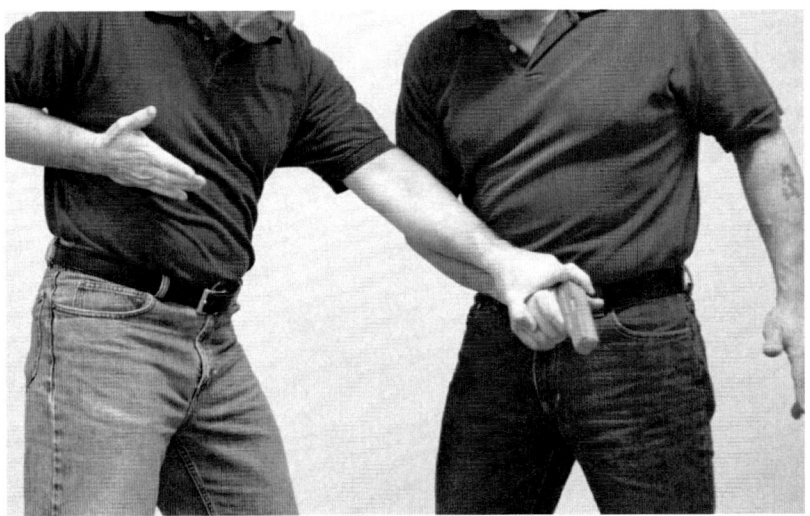

The defender clears by pushing the handgun away.

Under the Gun

The assailant presents a handgun to the defender's torso.

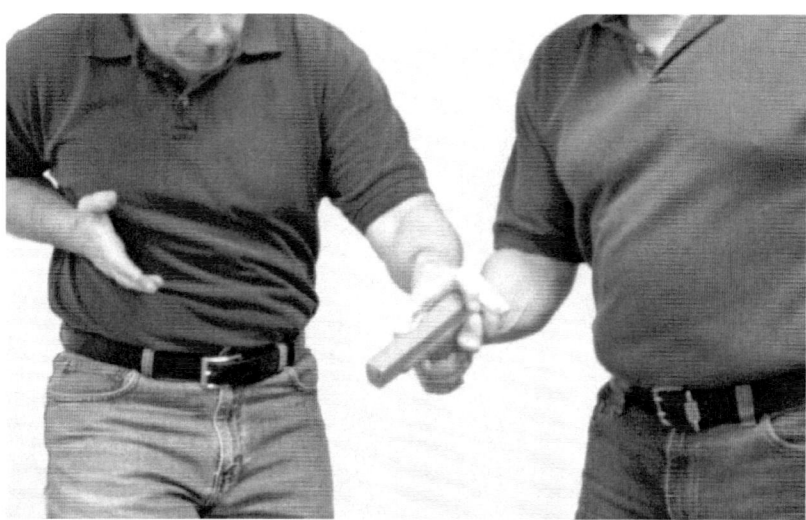

The defender clears by simultaneously snapping his body sideways and pushing the gun away.

Principles and Concepts

Those in the other camp will tell you that if you clear to the inside, you can be struck by your opponent's other hand, or you can be wrapped up and forced to grapple with a man with a gun.

Both sides have valid arguments. The bottom line is this: Whether you clear to the inside or the outside will be dictated by the circumstances and by the environment when and where you are attacked. If you are walking with your spouse, she is to your right, and you are attacked by a right-handed gunman, you cannot clear to the outside line. If you do, you may send a bullet toward her if the gun discharges (remember the 90 percent statistic). Likewise, if you are employed to protect a dignitary and are walking to his right front as part of a four man close protection detail, and the same right-handed gunman comes along and mistakenly points his gun at you instead of the dignitary, you cannot clear to the inside line. If you do and the weapon discharges, I hope you were paid in advance.

The bottom line, once more, is this: You must be able to clear effectively to *either* direction.

One final note on clearing: You must train yourself not to block the gun. Blocking, contrary to what some in the martial arts community will tell you, does not usually injure your opponent's arm. What it does do is repel the offending limb, moving it away from you. When you do this you have to chase the gun hand and try to gain control of it. This gives your opponent an opportunity to regroup, step back to a retention position, and shoot you as you flail the air trying to catch his hand. The right way to clear is to slap, stick, and grab.

The next step in the formula is control. Our goal at this stage is to control the muzzle of the weapon so it is not brought back onto us. This should occur almost simultaneously with a clear.

If you are performing an empty-hand disarm you will want both hands on the gun/gun hand in an opposing grip. In other words, the fingers of one hand will point to the sky and the fingers of the other hand will point to the ground.

The assailant presents a handgun to the defender's torso.

The defender has cleared incorrectly, blocking the gun away, and cannot control the muzzle. This allows the attacker to regroup

Grabbing the gun/hand with an opposing grip is safest because it prevents your attacker from rotating the weapon to dislodge your grip and retain the weapon.

Principles and Concepts

The assailant presents a handgun to the defender's torso.

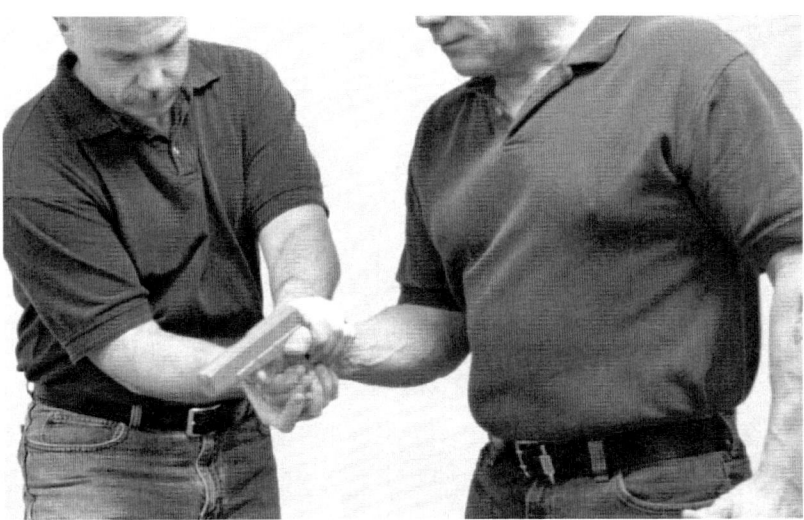

The defender has cleared to the outside line and now controls the direction of the muzzle with both hands.

Under the Gun

The assailant presents a handgun to the defender's torso.

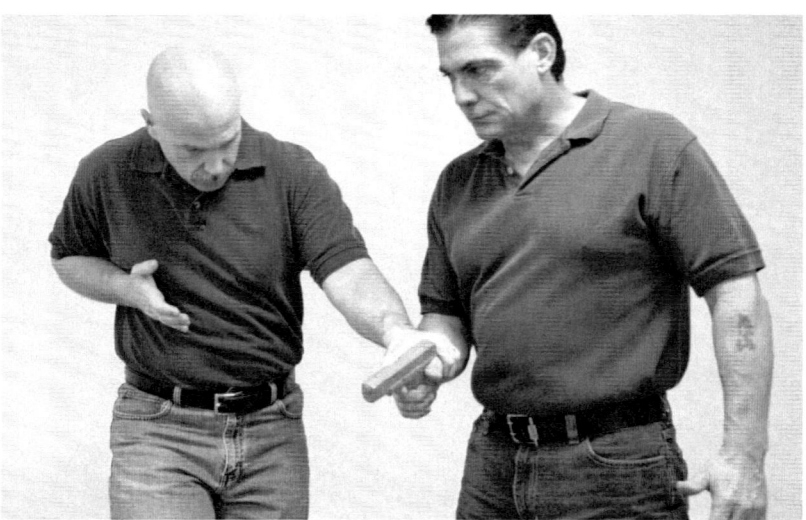

The defender has cleared to the outside line and controls the direction of the muzzle using one hand.

Principles and Concepts

Once the weapon is controlled, the next step is the actual disarm. We will cover these in detail later. You are encouraged to develop several that work for you. As much as possible, you should choose techniques that employ the same gross motor

Example of an opposing grip.

skills to ensure success under stress. Some techniques, however, will be specialty moves that are designed to work under specific conditions, such as disarming an assailant who is presenting a weapon to you while holding it horizontally.

The final step in the formula is to disable your attacker. This will mean different things to different people. Military personnel in a combat zone are under different rules of engagement than are law enforcement officers or civilians. As a general guideline, let us say that disabling your attacker renders him unable or unwilling to continue the fight. He may run away, he may be down with a disabling injury, or you may have had to shoot him to the ground when he attempted to take his weapon back after you disarmed him. When you plan your training, you must take into account all the possibilities you may face and work them into your scenarios.

ENDNOTES
1. John Farnam. Defense Training International Basic and Intermediate Defensive Handgun Course. 2004.
2. Ibid.
3. Ibid.

chapter 3

Training Evolutions

When you begin your training you should do so with a dummy gun. These are available from a variety of vendors, such as Ring's Blue Guns and Asp's Red Guns. They are usually constructed of some type of heavy plastic or hard rubber and mimic the look and feel of a real firearm. They cannot, however, be loaded or fired. During this phase of training the only safety gear you may need are mats to fall on and gloves for your hands. Many of the disarm techniques tend to scuff both partners' hands; wearing gloves will allow you to keep training without having to stop and go to the first aid kit for bandages.

One modification you may wish to make to the dummy gun is to cut the trigger guard away and sand the ends smooth. Some of the techniques will lever the trigger guard back against the trigger finger to break it. Removing the trigger guard will allow you to train while saving wear and tear on your partners.

Initial training with gloves and an inert dummy gun.

Stress inoculations begin; note use of eye protection. The trainer used is a pistol equipped with a conversion kit that fires a marking cartridge.

Training Evolutions

Initially, concentrate on proper body movements during the techniques. Start slowly and gradually increase speed. One thing that is not recommended is to do the techniques by the numbers. For example, movement number one would simply be to clear and hold, movement number two would be to control, and so on. Don't do each technique this way. Instead, move slowly but smoothly through the entire technique. This gives better results in the long run. Initially, your partner should cooperate and allow you to disarm him. As your skill increases, he should begin resisting your attempts and try to retain his weapon. Some examples of this would be trying to pull back and away as you begin a disarm, slapping you with his support hand, or grabbing and jostling you and using a variety of verbal commands that a robbery suspect might use. Vary these. Some suspects keep things very quiet and low key, while others are more animated.

The next phase of the training begins the stress inoculations. The dummy gun is replaced with an Airsoft training pistol that fires plastic pellets. There are two types of these on the market today. One is a single-shot model of all-plastic construction. It is relatively inexpensive, but these models tend to break quickly as the training tempo increases. A better model, although more expensive, has a steel slide and uses compressed gas to fire in a semiautomatic mode. These are more realistic and tend to hold up to the stresses of training better than do their single-shot cousins. When using these trainers, eye protection is mandatory for everyone in the training area.

You may wish to wrap your throat and wear a heavy sweatshirt along with protective gloves. You can complete all further training evolutions with this equipment.

For those who have access to them, there is equipment that goes a step beyond these trainers. You can use a real firearm that has been altered with a conversion kit that replaces the barrel, allowing it to fire a special marking cartridge and making it unable to fire a standard projectile. The advantage to using this equipment is that stress levels approach those experienced in the real world. This is as real as you can get without being shot at with live ammunition. The disadvantages are that more safety equipment is required (full face shields, chest protectors, throat guards, a cup and supporter) for everyone in the training area.

The marking cartridges typically travel between 250 and 500 feet per second and can cause real injuries. The equipment is also expensive to purchase and some manufacturers limit the purchase to military and law enforcement.

When you move to using a trainer that actually fires a projectile, two things change. The first, as already discussed, is the use of more personal protective equipment. The second is that when you begin working the techniques again, your partner will now cooperate as he did with the dummy gun evolution with one exception: When you move to clear the muzzle, he will fire. If you don't clear properly, if you telegraph your movement, or if you make any other kind of mistake, you'll know it immediately. As you improve, your partner will add resistance as he did with the dummy gun evolution until you are performing scenario work against an aggressor rather than practicing static techniques.

One word of warning at the beginning stage of this evolution: You must guard against getting into a rhythm when working repetitions of the techniques. During one training session I observed, one partner got into the habit of clearing on every third breath after the gun was presented. The partner who was acting the part of the "bad guy" either consciously or unconsciously picked up on this and successfully shot the "good guy" every time. This obviously didn't do much to enhance the defender's confidence in his abilities. A few times with a coach watching closely corrected the problem, but not until after the defender had a nicely grouped set of welts on his chest.

Training Evolutions

Another thing to guard against in this or any other force-on-force training is turning the exercise into an overgrown game of tag. The goal here is to build skill. When people begin gaming up the training so they can make a point, the training suffers. Those playing the role of the bad guy need to be carefully instructed as to what they can and cannot do during both technique practice and scenarios. If this seems artificial, consider that the bad guy in this case knows what the defender is going to do before he does it. That alone is a huge advantage. In real life, an assailant won't have that edge. If you are in charge of the training, you need to make the scenarios winnable if the defender does everything right. We do not want to reward bad habits, but at the same time, giving our trainees unwinnable scenarios does nothing but teach them to lose.

As the training progresses to scenario work, several things need to be added beyond the use of projectile trainers and safety gear. The first thing is to practice delivering verbal distractions. If you don't practice this in training, it will not happen in a real, high-stress situation.

The second thing that you must practice is clearing a general malfunction once you've gained control of the opponent's firearm. If faced with multiple attackers, or if your opponent attacks you in an attempt to regain his weapon after the disarm is successful, the captured gun may be the only weapon you have to fight with. Remember, the gun is likely to discharge during a disarming attempt. It will probably have three to four hands on it when it does (his and yours). The odds are very good that a malfunction will be induced if it is a semiautomatic pistol. You may have to clear the malfunction in order to use the weapon against your attacker(s).

The recommended procedure to clear a malfunctioning semiautomatic pistol is known as "tap/roll/rack." After you have secured the attacker's weapon, continue to move laterally off the line of force. Attain a firing grip on the weapon and tap the base of the magazine with your support hand to ensure that it is seated. Next, bring your support hand over the top rear of the slide and rack it briskly. As you do this, roll the pistol to the right to help clear the ejection port and chamber of the pistol.

After securing a firing grip, tap the base of the magazine with your support hand to ensure that it is seated.

Next, grasp the rear of the slide with an overhand grip.

Rack the slide and roll the ejection port toward the ground.

Begin presenting the pistol to your attacker.

The original version of this technique did not include the roll or flip to the side to help clear the round. Some may wonder why it is recommended that you do so in this case. Any handgun used for defensive/combative purposes should be able to live-eject a round. In plain English, with a round in the chamber and a loaded magazine inserted, you should be able to cycle the slide manually and have the loaded rounds eject without hanging up. If you carry a handgun, you need to make sure that your pistol does this. The problem is that in this instance you are not using *your* pistol, you're using someone else's and you won't have time to test it for this function. In this case you need to stack the deck in your favor any way you can.

With a little practice this maneuver can be completed in under a second while maintaining visual contact with the attacker. Once the gun is up and running again, you need to scan, breathe, and assess the situation.

When training, your partner has three options at this point. He can turn as if to run, he can go to the ground as if disabled or surrendering, or he can attack again and try to regain his weapon. You need to practice against each of these three possibilities.

WHAT TO DO AFTERWARD

The final thing that needs to be practiced during training is what to do with your assailant's gun after you've disarmed him. Some of you may be tempted to keep the weapon as a war trophy. After all, you worked hard to get it. Don't give in to this temptation. You have to turn the gun over to the authorities. The gun will likely be stolen. If your assailant tried using the gun against you he probably did the same to others. You may be holding evidence to a murder. If you decide to keep your trophy it may very well come back to bite you in the future.

Your immediate options will depend on your situation. Your first action should be to clear the area. Your attacker may have accomplices in the area who may come to check on him. If he ran away during the altercation, he may have gone for reinforcements.

Leaving the gun at the scene is irresponsible. Somebody will likely find it before the police can get to it. Whether that somebody is another criminal or a child, this is a bad thing. If you don't want to take the gun with you, clear the weapon and drop it in the nearest storm sewer. If you don't know how to clear it, or don't have time to clear it, drop it in the sewer anyway. If it does discharge the round will have the best chance of being contained, it will be difficult for others to get to the weapon, and storm sewers don't move, so it will be easy to tell the authorities where they can recover the weapon. If you have to or choose to take the weapon with you, first clear it if you know how (but don't try if you don't know

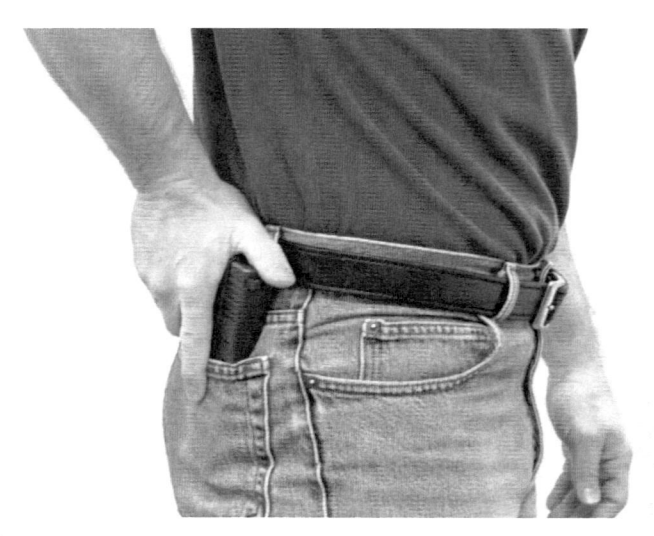

If you have to take the pistol with you, place it muzzle down in your back pocket.

how). After you've cleared the weapon, place the weapon muzzle-down in a rear pants pocket as you keep your finger off the trigger and outside the trigger guard. This way, if you do have a negligent discharge you are less likely to sustain serious injury.

The decision of how you will turn the weapon over to the authorities is yours. The only thing I will tell you is, do not keep it as a souvenir.

chapter 4

Empty-Hand Responses: Frontal Attacks

Now we'll cover empty-hand responses. As stated in the section describing training evolutions, begin slowly but smoothly. As your skill increases, insert stressors. Begin using a trainer such as an Airsoft gun that fires a nonlethal projectile. Add movement and verbalization, both from you and your training partner. Keep your scenarios realistic yet winnable if the defender does everything right. The techniques shown are certainly not the only ones out there. They are ones that have worked consistently during training evolutions for a wide variety of trainees. The photo sequences will show techniques from front and rear attacks. The same techniques can also be used against attacks from the side, on either high or low lines with minor modifications.

ONE-HAND HOLD

The attacker presents a handgun to the defender's torso from the front.

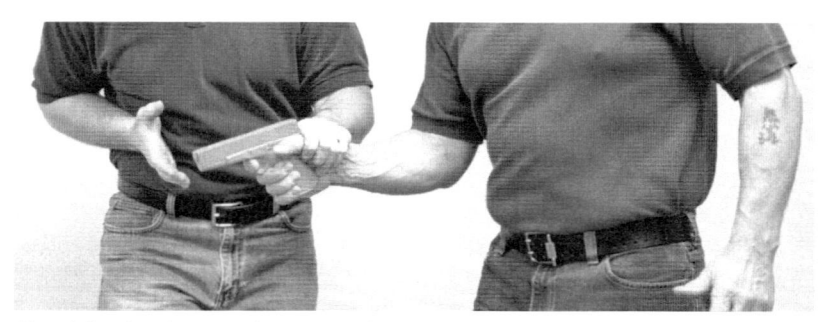

The defender clears to the outside line.

The defender grasps the attacker's gun and hand in a two-hand opposing grip and begins to turn the weapon back toward the attacker.

Empty-Hand Responses: Frontal Attacks

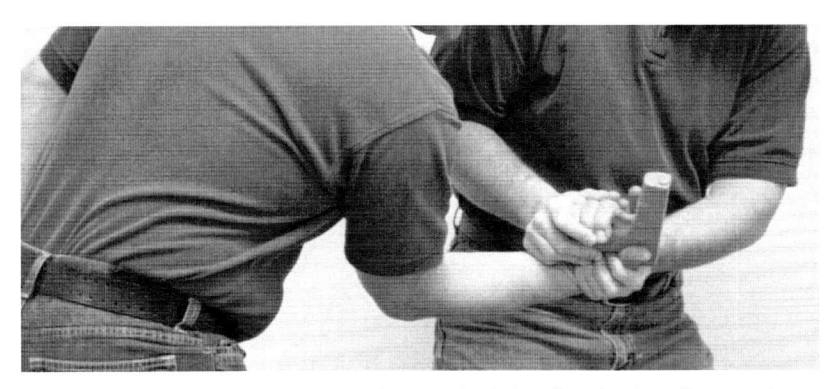

The defender simultaneously turns the attacker's hand and points the muzzle outward. Note the change in camera angle for clarity.

The defender has taken the attacker to the ground. From here he will remove the weapon and follow up as appropriate for the operational conditions.

ONE-HAND HOLDS

The attacker presents a handgun to the defender's torso from the front.

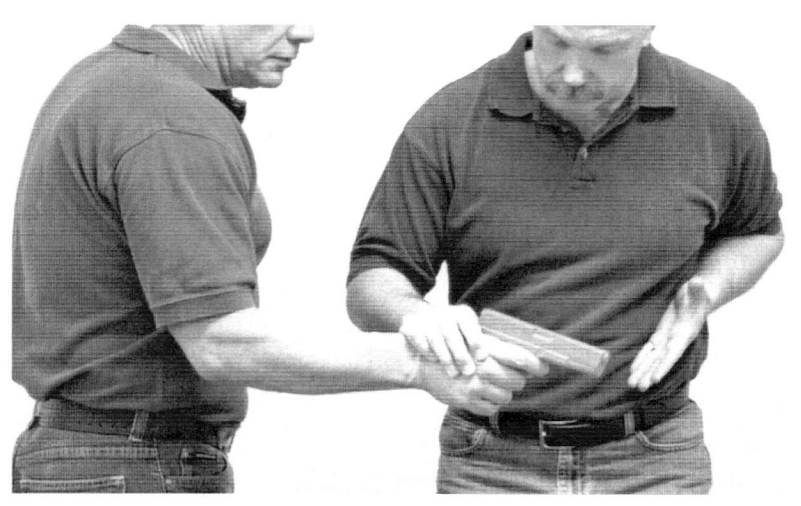

The defender clears to the inside line.

Empty-Hand Responses: Frontal Attacks

The defender controls using a two-hand grip. He pushes the barrel of the handgun back toward the attacker, keeping the barrel of the weapon parallel with the attacker's forearm.

The defender rips the attacker's weapon out of his hand. Once the barrel is pointed back at the attacker and brings the weapon back to a retention position as he performs a malfunction clearance and moves off the line of force.

The attacker presents a handgun to the defender's front torso.

The defender clears and controls to the outside line.

Empty-Hand Responses: Frontal Attacks

The defender begins punching the barrel of the weapon back toward the attacker.

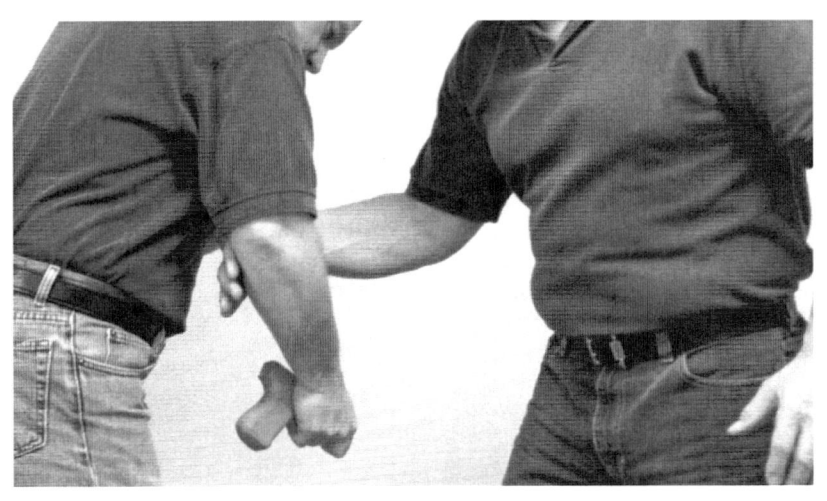

The defender rips the weapon down and out of the attacker's grip, using the barrel as a lever. He will then make distance and move off the line of force as he attains a firing grip on the weapon and performs a general malfunction clearance.

Under the Gun

The attacker presents a handgun to the defender, holding it horizontally.

The defender has the option, in this case, to clear to either side. Here he moves to the outside line, controlling the muzzle with a two-hand opposing grip.

Empty-Hand Responses: Frontal Attacks

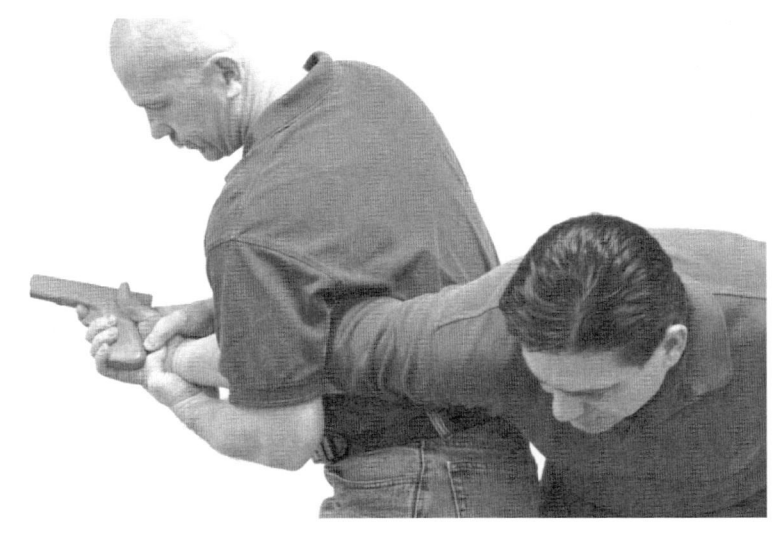

The defender locks the attacker's elbow in his armpit and breaks the elbow by simultaneously shearing it up and sideways.

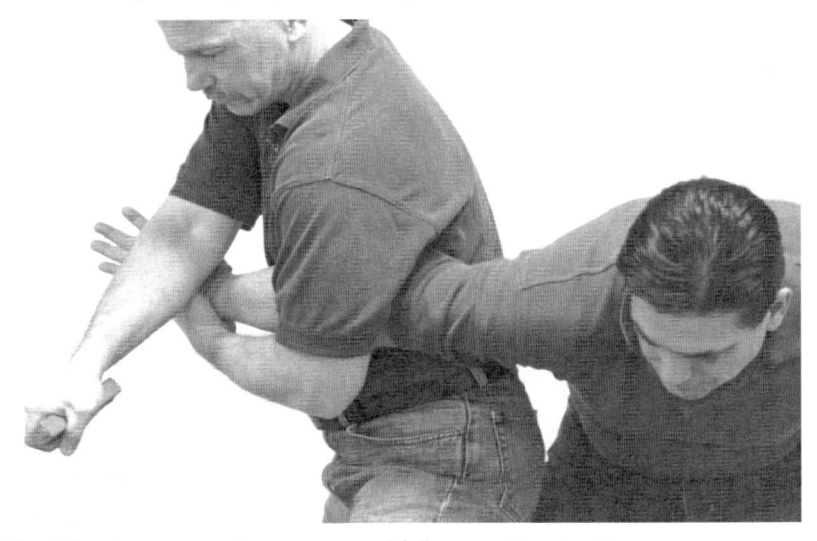

The defender removes the weapon and follows up as necessary.

Under the Gun

The attacker presents a handgun to the defender's face.

The defender simultaneously drops low and clears straight up.

Empty-Hand Responses: Frontal Attacks

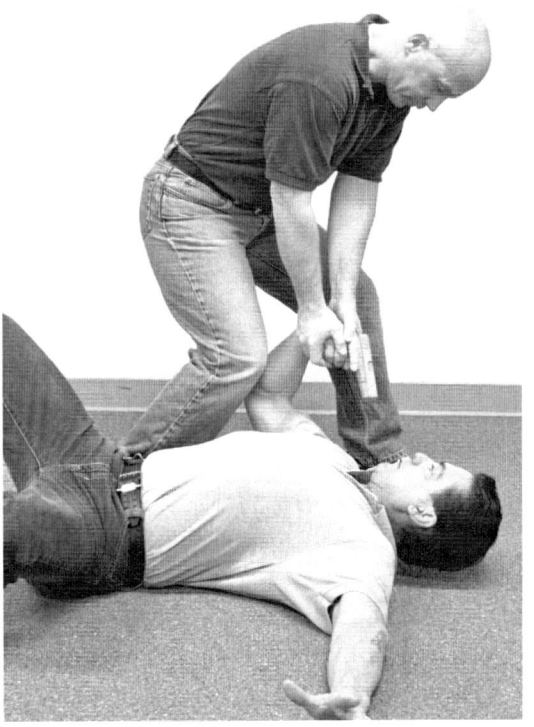

Above: The defender applies a reverse wristlock

Left: The defender takes the attacker to the ground, removes the weapon, and follows up as necessary.

TWO-HAND HOLD

In this case, the defender does not have a choice regarding how he clears. He *must* clear to the outside line of the attacker's gun hand. If the defender attempts to clear to the inside line of the weapon, he will slap the attacker's support hand. This will give the attacker an opportunity to retract the weapon to a retention position and fire.

The attacker presents a handgun to the defender in a two-hand hold.

Empty-Hand Responses: Frontal Attacks

The defender clears and controls the outside line of the weapon hand.

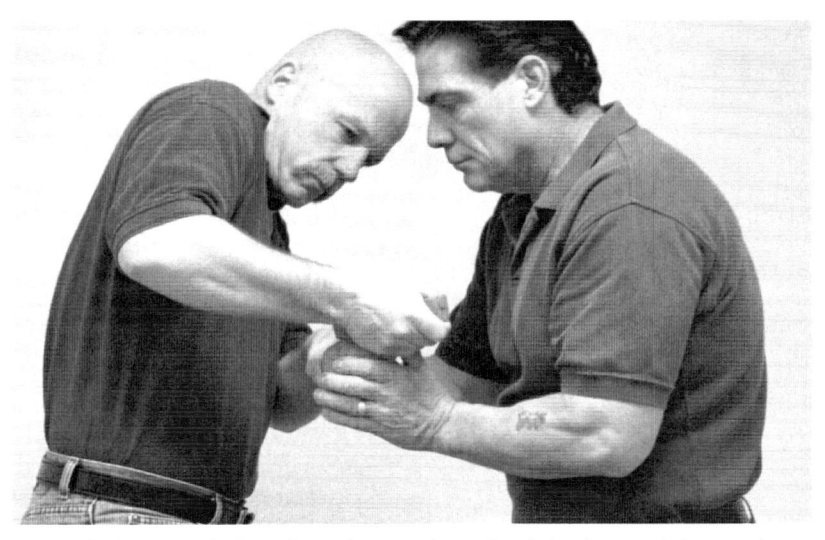

The defender uses the barrel as a lever and punches it back toward the attacker.

Under the Gun

The defender removes the weapon, ripping it down and out of the attacker's grip. He will then make distance, moving off the line of force as he attains a firing grip and performs a general malfunction clearance.

chapter 5

Empty-Hand Responses: Rear Attacks

Disarming an attacker who has a gun to your back is extremely risky. You need to take a few extra things into account prior to attempting this. As stated before, the only time you should attempt this for real is if the only other choice is to be shot.

First, you must be able to feel the gun. If you cannot feel the muzzle against your body, then you are too far away to attempt a disarm. Second, try to see the gun before you move. This can be hidden in the natural act of looking to see what is jabbing you in the back. If your attacker has grabbed you with his empty hand, you will have to wait to move. If you don't, he will feel you as you begin to clear, jam the effort, and shoot you. If you can, talk to your attacker in an effort to turn and face him and *then* disarm him. When clearing, take care not to strike the gun. Bump it off target as you turn or you will have the same problem we discussed earlier concerning blocking the gun during the clearing phase.

Under the Gun

The attacker presents a handgun to the defender's back.

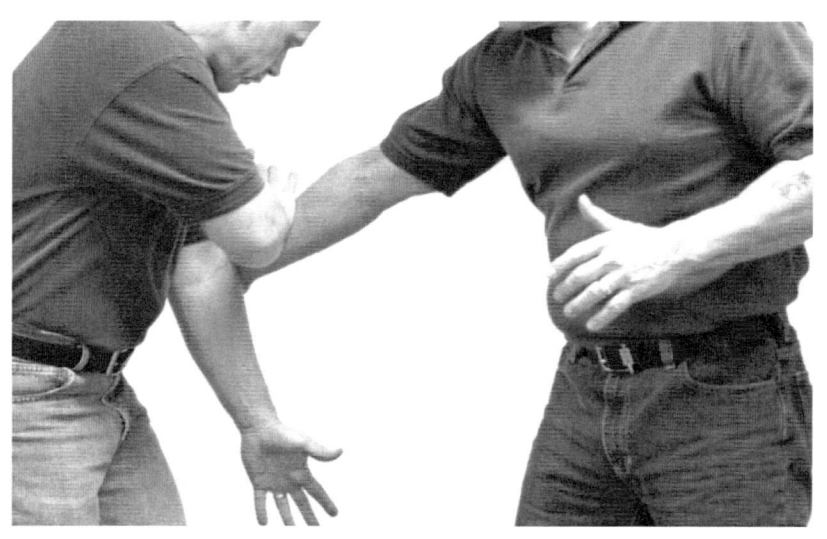

The defender spins to the inside and bumps the gun to clear.

Empty-Hand Responses: Rear Attacks

The defender controls as he continues to move to face the attacker.

The defender strips the weapon by punching the barrel parallel with the attacker's forearm and back toward him.

Under the Gun

The defender moves off the line of force, performs a malfunction clearance, and assesses.

Empty-Hand Responses: Rear Attacks

The attacker presents a handgun to the defender's back.

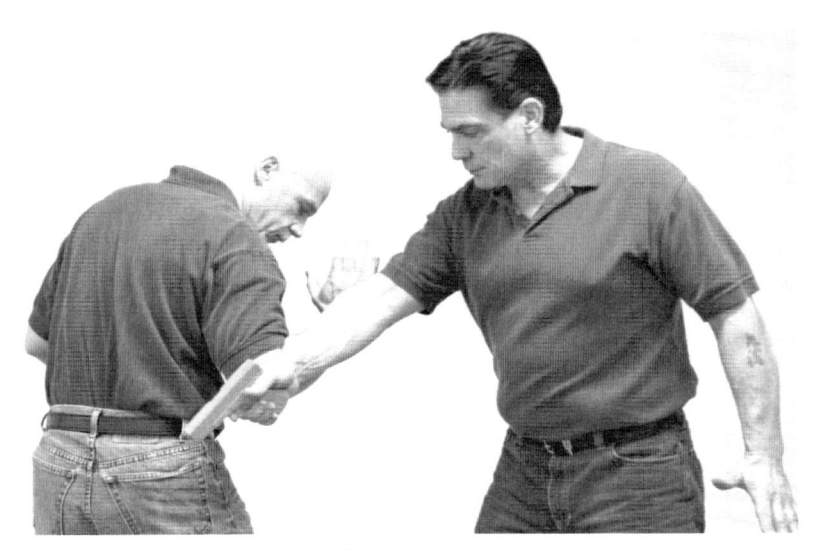

The defender spins to the outside line, bumping the gun to clear.

The defender grasps the attacker's arm at the wrist, jerking the elbow straight.

The defender steps in front of the attacker's legs and brings the attacker's elbow tight against his upper arm.

The defender snaps the attacker's arm across his body to break the attacker's elbow.

Empty-Hand Responses: Rear Attacks

The defender continues his motion, taking the attacker to the ground.

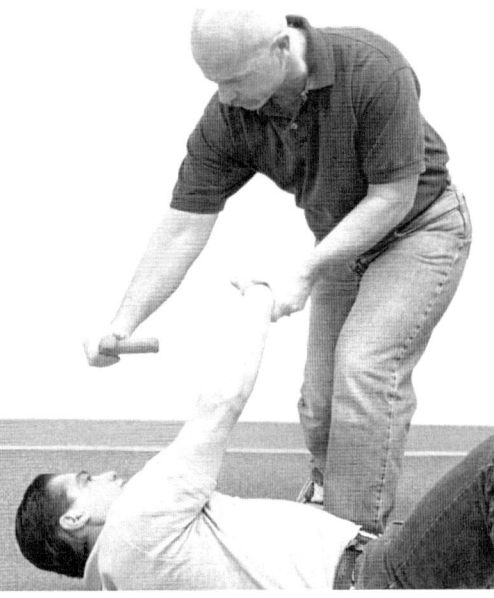

The defender removes the weapon and follows up as necessary.

The attacker presents a handgun to the defender's back.

The defender spins to the outside and bumps the gun to clear.

The defender continues his motion to face his attacker.

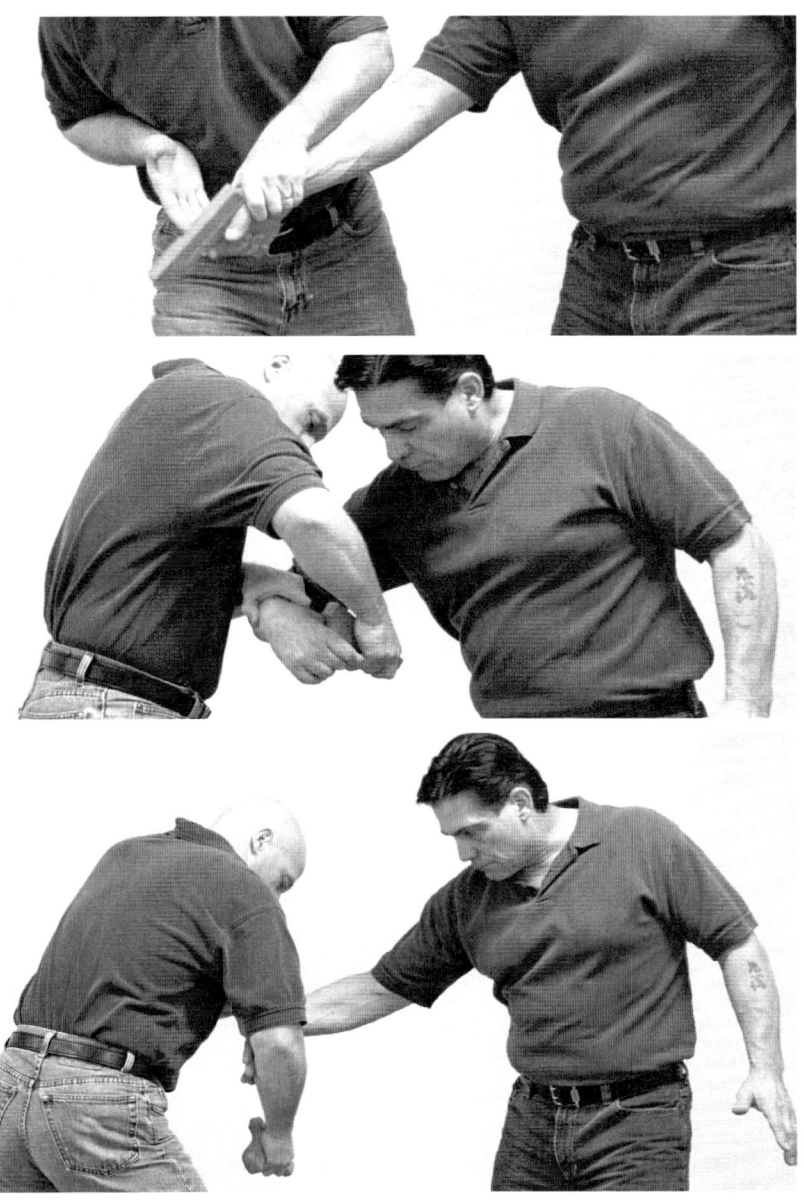

The defender begins stripping the weapon by using the barrel as a lever and punching back toward the attacker, parallel with the attacker's forearm. Once the muzzle is pointed back at the attacker, the barrel is punched down and the weapon removed from the attacker's grip. The defender will then move off the line of force while attaining a firing grip and performing a general malfunction clearance.

Under the Gun

The attacker presents a handgun to the defender's back.

The defender spins to the outside, bumping the gun to clear.

Empty-Hand Responses: Rear Attacks

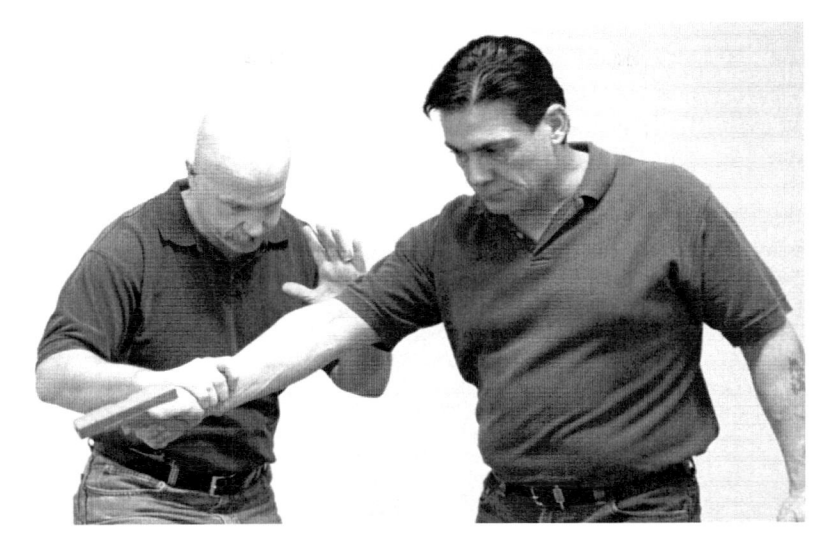

The defender moves down the attacker's arm.

The defender grasps the attacker's wrist with one hand and begins locking the attacker's elbow with his forearm.

The defender sets the lock and drives the attacker to the ground.

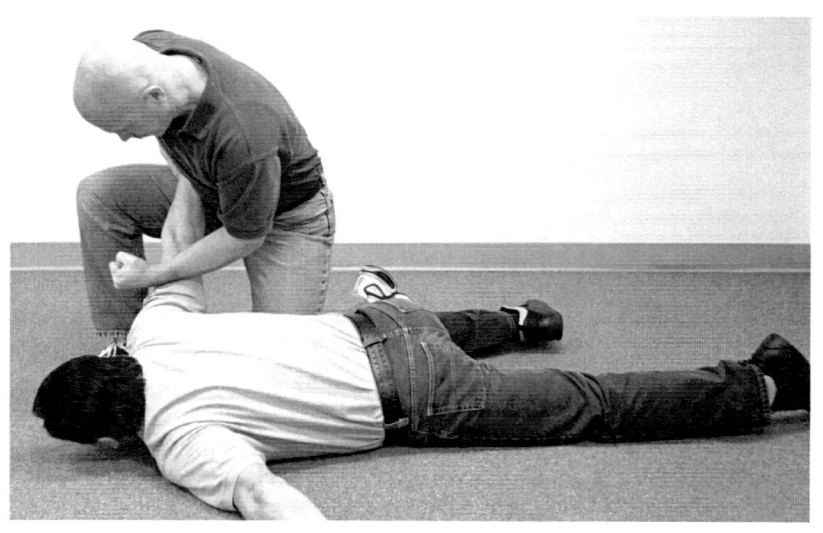

The defender has the attacker on the ground, removes the weapon, and follows up as necessary.

Empty-Hand Responses: Rear Attacks

The attacker presents a handgun to the defender's back.

The defender spins to the outside and bumps the gun to clear.

The defender reaches over and grasps the attacker's gun hand as he maintains contact with the attacker's forearm with his other hand.

The defender grasps the attacker's gun and hand in a two-hand opposing grip.

The defender begins simultaneously turning the attacker's hand in and outward to lock the wrist. Note the change of camera angle for clarity.

Empty-Hand Responses: Rear Attacks

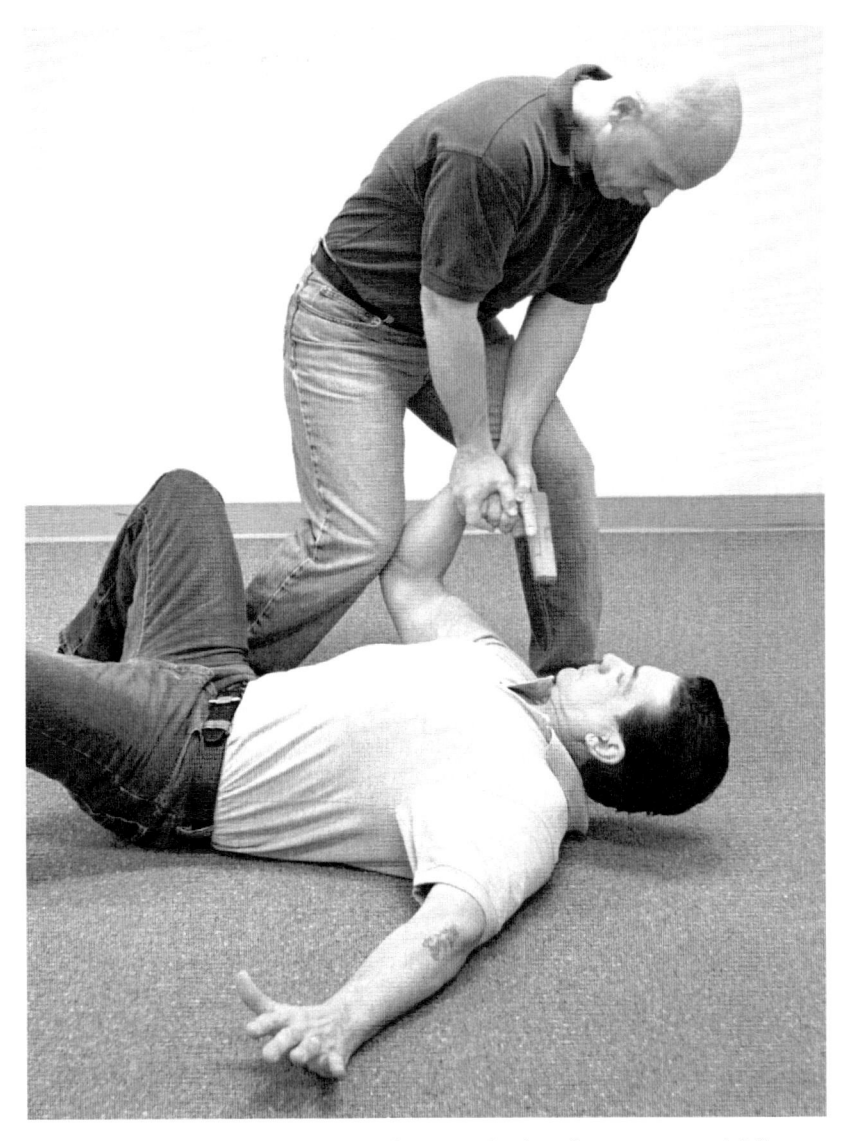

The defender sends the attacker to the ground, takes the weapon, and follows up as necessary.

chapter 6

Armed Responses

Ideally, you do not want to face an armed attacker without a weapon of your own. Weapons are force multipliers, and not availing ourselves of them when facing armed attackers is foolish. I am going to presume that you have your legal ducks in a row if you are going around armed.

We are going to look at responses using a tactical folding knife, a fixed-blade knife, and our own handgun. The basic principles of disarming do not change; we are merely changing the mechanics of dealing with the problem. We must first deal with the weapon that is pointed at us—Clear. We then have to keep that muzzle from tracking back onto us—Control. We then have to take the weapon away from our attacker—Disarm. Finally, we have to keep the attacker from mounting a counterattack against us—Disable. If you attempt to change this order or disregard it merely because you have a weapon of your own, you will likely be shot at close quarters.

The examples shown do not have the defender drawing from concealment. This was done for the sake of clarity. In your own training, if you carry concealed, train to draw and deploy your weapon that way.

ARMED WITH A KNIFE

Tactical Folding Knife

If you are carrying some type of tactical folding knife, there are some things you must consider. These are how you will carry the knife and how you will open it. It is recommended that you carry your folder in the front waistband of your pants. This allows you easy access to the knife with a minimum of shoulder movement using either hand. The second consideration, how you will open the knife, will come into sharp focus when you begin your training evolutions. Under stress you may find that using the hole, disc or stud to thumb the blade open does not work as well as you thought it might. It is highly recommended that you learn some method of inertial opening and make sure that it works with your particular carry knife. Because the draw will be slower, you may wish to insert a finger jab to the eyes as you clear and control as a distraction prior to deploying the blade. Another option is to keep the knife closed initially and use it as an impact weapon, like a pocket stick.

You also don't want to try to clear, control, and deploy the knife simultaneously. I have found in training that often, when this is attempted, the knife goes sailing off into space. One final note: If you do lose control of your knife during a disarm, or you cannot deploy the blade either in training or real life, jettison the knife and default to an empty-hand disarm. Do not stand there trying to snap the blade out. It's not helping you, so get rid of it and get back in the fight!

Armed Responses

The attacker presents a handgun to the defender's torso from the front.

The defender clears to the outside line, controlling the muzzle with one hand.

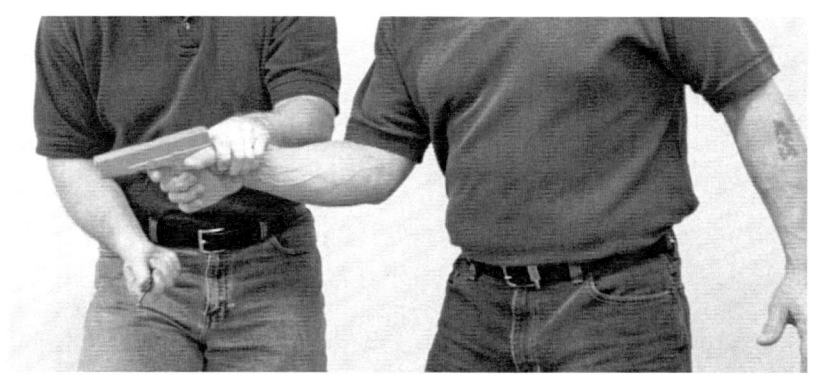

The defender accesses his tactical folder and opens it inertially, keeping the knife close to his body.

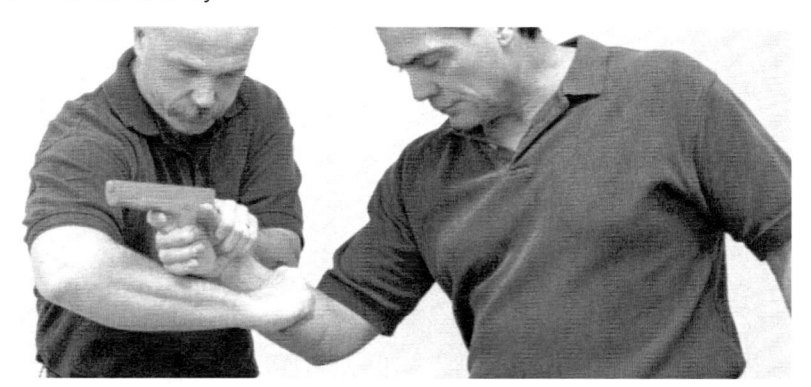

The defender slices the inside of the attacker's forearm, starting at the top (radial) side and cutting down. He targets the radial nerve and flexor muscle groups and tendons.

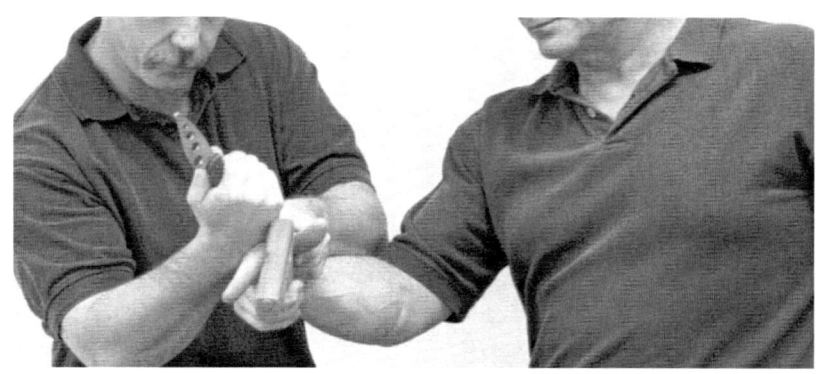

The defender ejects the handgun using the back of his hand.

Armed Responses

The defender slides his leg behind the attacker's while thrusting his arm across the attacker's body to begin a cross-body takedown.

Under the Gun

The takedown completed, the defender follows up as necessary.

Armed Responses

The attacker presents a handgun to the defender's front torso.

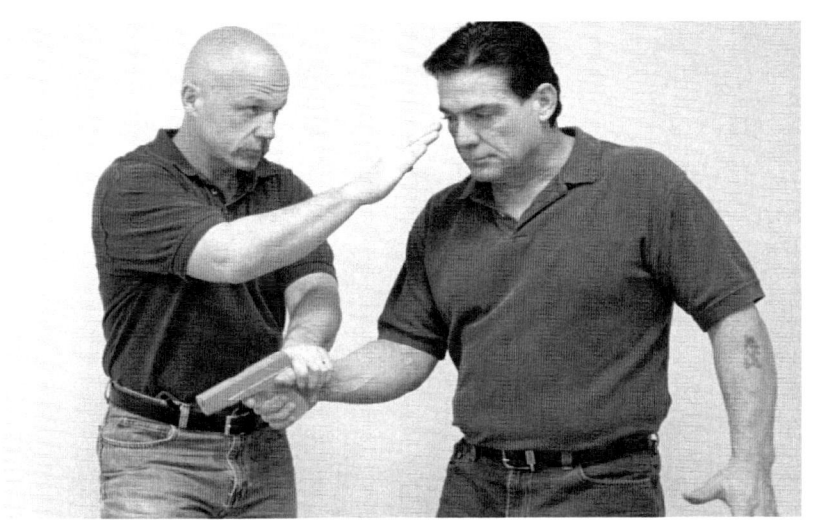

The defender clears to the outside line, controlling with one hand and attacking the eyes with a finger jab.

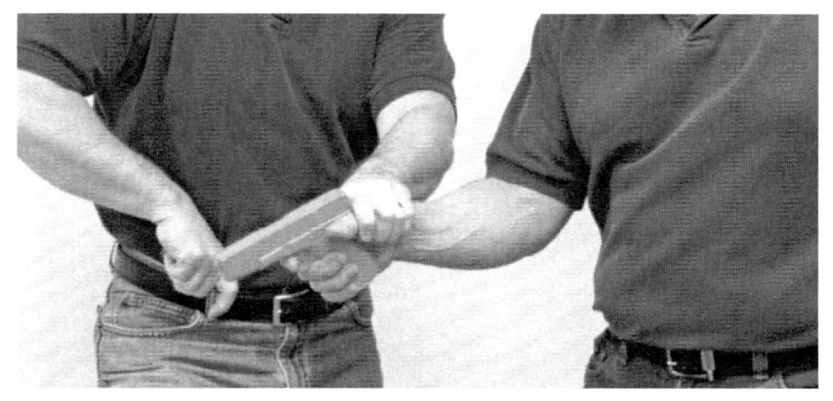

The defender accesses his tactical folder.

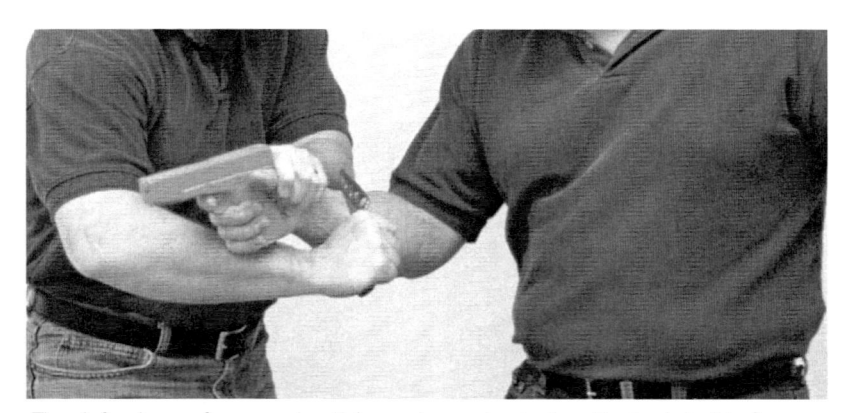

The defender performs an inertial opening and cuts the attacker's inside forearm, targeting the radial nerve and flexor muscles.

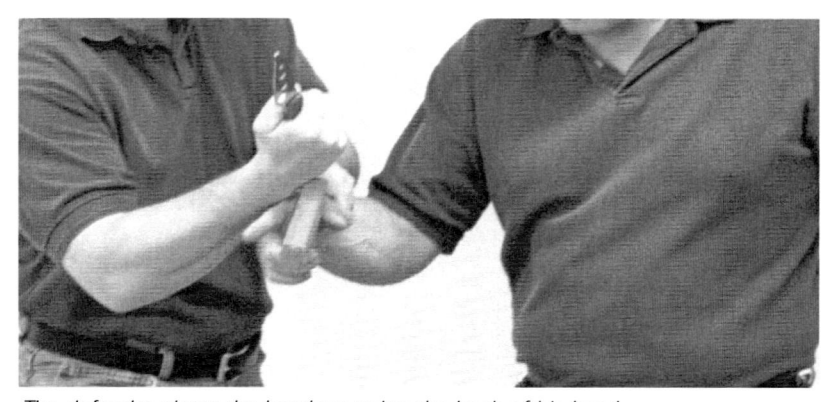

The defender ejects the handgun using the back of his hand.

Armed Responses

The defender takes the attacker to the ground using a cross-body takedown.

The defender assesses, following up as necessary.

71

Under the Gun

The attacker presents a handgun to the defender's front torso.

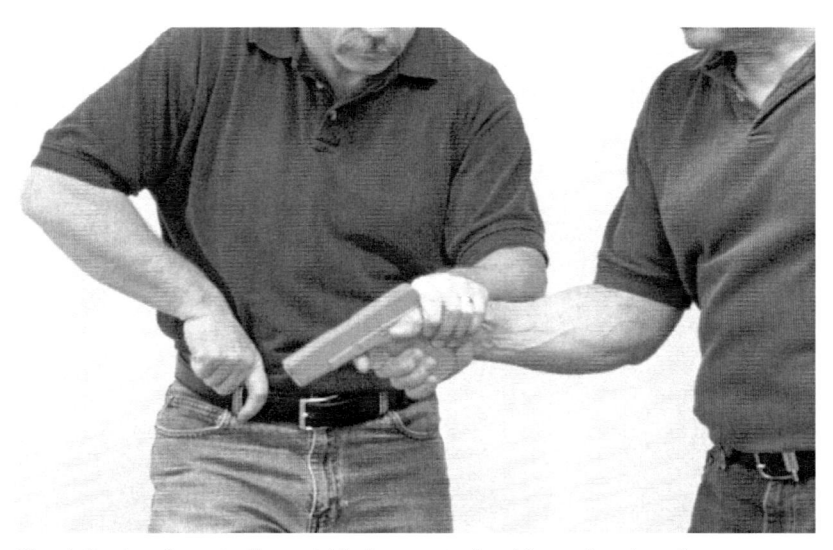

The defender clears to the outside line, controls with one hand, and accesses his tactical folder.

Armed Responses

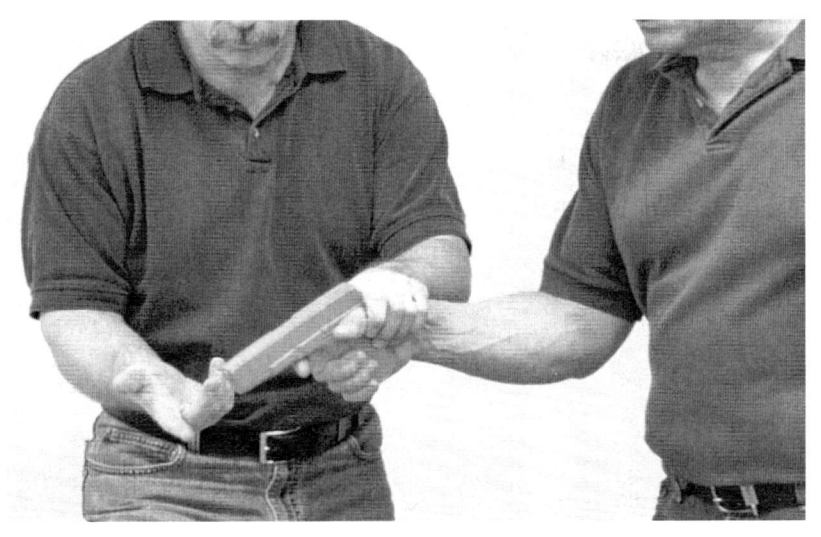

The defender either drops his knife or cannot get it opened.

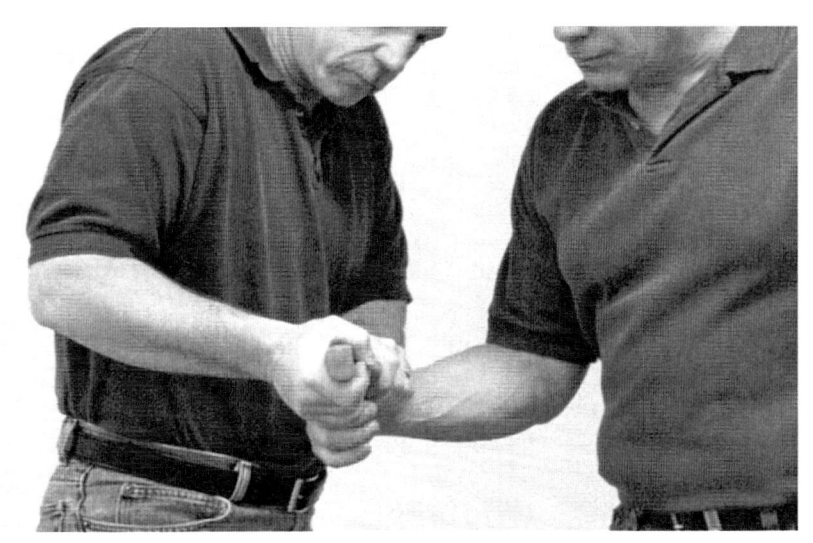

The defender immediately defaults to an empty-hand disarm, in this case an outside strip.

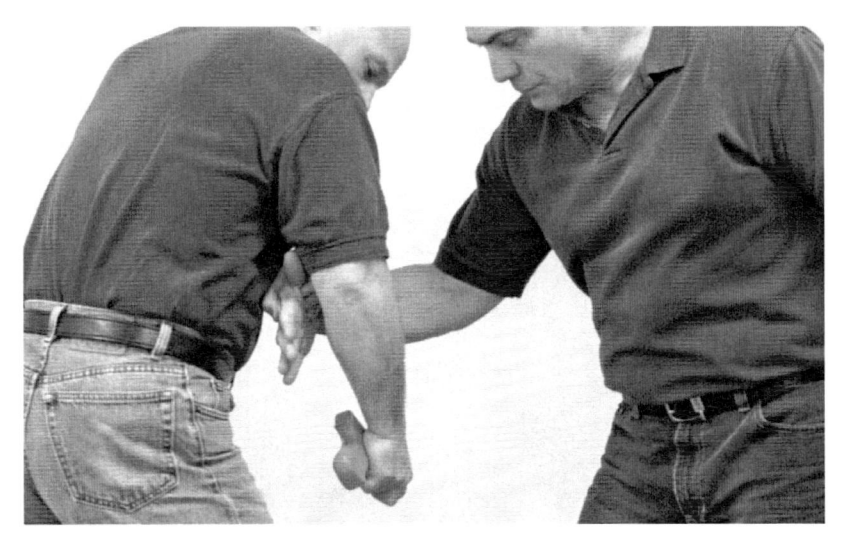

The defender punches the barrel of the weapon back toward the attacker and parallel with the attacker's forearm. He completes the disarm by ripping the weapon down and out. He will then move off the line of force, attain a firing grip, and perform a general malfunction clearance.

Fixed Blade Knife

If you carry a fixed-blade knife it is recommended that the knife be sheathed on the strong side of the body somewhere between the belt buckle and where the outside seam of a pair of jeans runs. The knife should be sheathed so that when drawn in a reverse grip the edge is in, or facing toward the defender's forearm/elbow. This will allow you to deploy the blade rapidly and with a minimum of shoulder movement.

Note that in this technique we are using the edge of the blade as opposed to the point. "Picking" a hand can be very effective, but in this case the opponent's hand will be covered by your own. Using the edge will give you a greater likelihood of success in this case.

Armed Responses

The attacker presents a handgun to the defender's front torso.

The defender clears to the outside line, controlling with one hand and accessing his fixed blade.

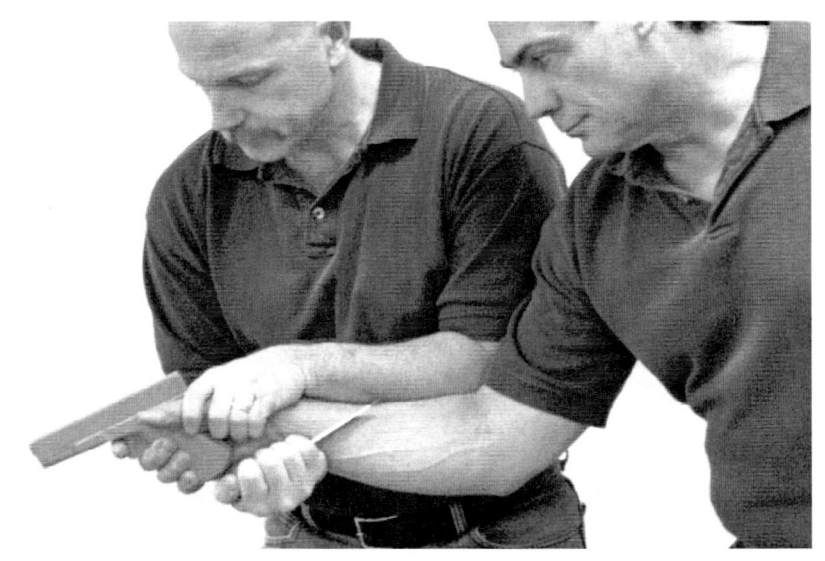

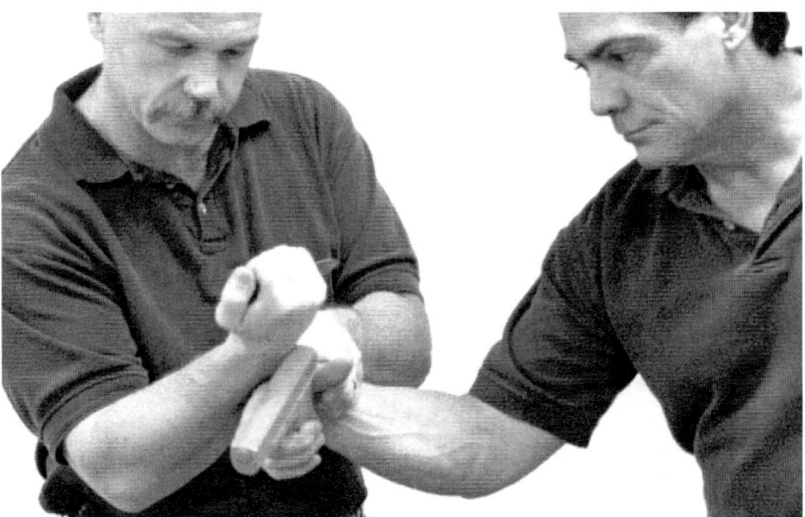

The defender brings his knife to the inside of the attacker's forearm and rips the edge down, targeting the radial nerve and flexor muscles. The defender ejects the pistol using the back of his hand.

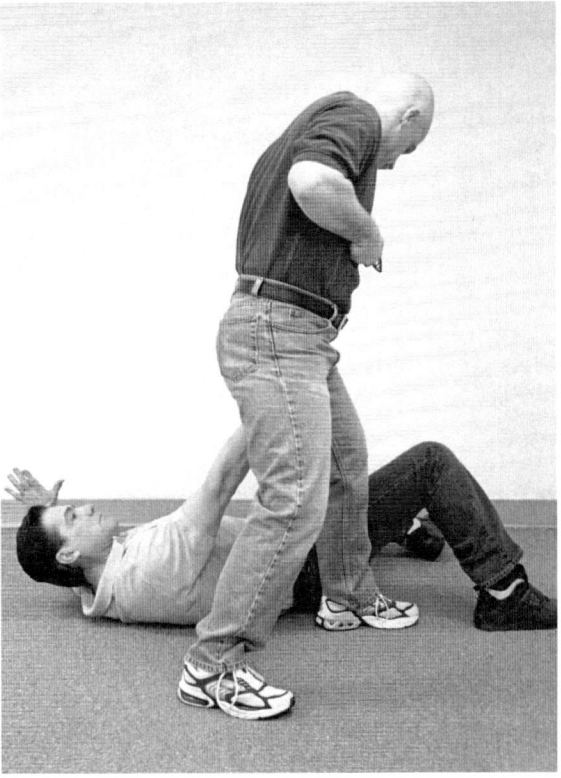

Above: The defender takes the attacker to the ground using a cross-body takedown.

Left: The defender assesses and follows up as necessary.

ARMED WITH A HANDGUN

When armed with a handgun, the same basic rules apply. There are two options. The first and safest is to perform an empty-hand disarm once you have control of the opponent's weapon, transfer his weapon to your support hand, present your own pistol, and follow up as necessary.

The attacker presents a handgun to the defender's front torso.

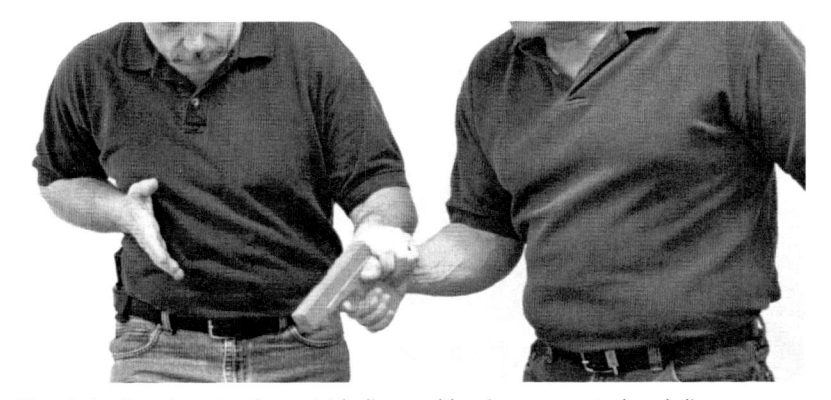

The defender clears to the outside line and begins an empty-hand disarm.

The defender punches the barrel of the weapon back toward the attacker and parallel with the attacker's forearm.

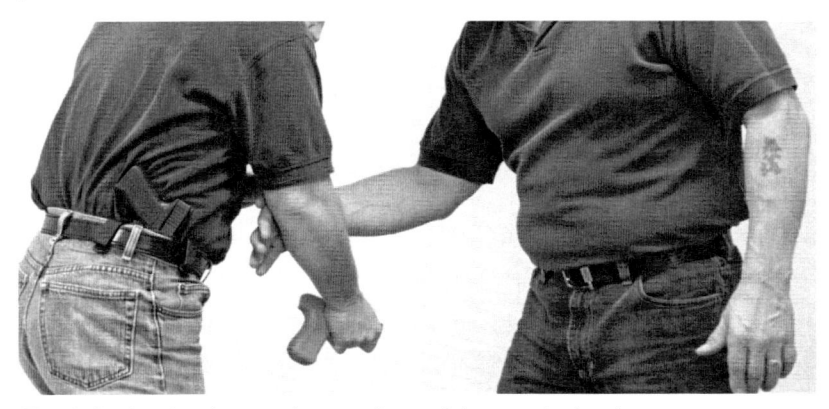

The defender rips the gun down and out of the attacker's grip.

Under the Gun

The defender transfers the attacker's weapon to his own support hand and makes distance, pushing the attacker away and moving off the line of force.

The defender has placed the attacker's weapon in a retention position and performs his own drawstroke. He covers the attacker from a retention position, issuing verbal commands at this point. He will then follow up as necessary.

Armed Responses

A second but slightly riskier option is to clear and control as you present your own firearm and shoot your assailant to the ground. This is much faster, but there is the added risk that you may shoot your own arm in the process. You must practice concerning which way you push the attacker's arm. If he is presenting his weapon to your body, you must push it low, to his opposite hip. If he is presenting to your face, you have to push the weapon high and across his body.

The attacker presents a handgun to the defender's front torso.

Under the Gun

The defender clears to the outside, controlling with one hand and pushing the attacker's weapon low toward the attacker's opposite hip as he accesses his own pistol.

The defender keeps pressure on the attacker's weapon hand and turns into him, keeping his own weapon in a retention position.

Armed Responses

The defender presents his own pistol fully and shoots the attacker to the ground, following up as necessary.

Under the Gun

The attacker presents a handgun to the defender's face.

The defender clears to the outside, controlling with one hand and pushing the attacker's weapon in the direction of the attacker's opposite shoulder as he accesses his own pistol.

Armed Responses

The defender presents his own pistol in a retention position and shoots the attacker to the ground, following up as necessary.

Conclusion

It is my sincere wish that you never need the skills described here. Reality being what it is, I also know that it is likely that some of you may not be so fortunate. If you cannot be safe, my wish for you is that you train hard, train smart, and prevail.

About the Author

James Miller is a retired police officer with 20 years of service, 17 of which were spent as an operator with a multi-jurisdictional SWAT team. He has been training in the martial arts for more than 30 years and holds black belts or equivalent rankings in several systems. He currently works with the tactical response team for a nuclear facility.